STEERAGE

BERT STERN

# STEERAGE

New and Collected Poems

Ibbetson Street Press 2009

*Published by:*

Ibbetson Street Press
25 School Street
Somerville, MA 02143

Book design by Michael Alpert. Cover artwork by Joan Braun.

Acknowledgments

I thank the editors of the following journals, where some of these poems or versions of them were originally published: *Poetry:* "A Little Poem," "Steerage"; New *Letters:* "A New Life"; *Indiana Review:* "Nobody Loves the Dead Enough"; *Rooted in Rock: New Adirondack Writing* (Syracuse University Press, 2001): "Early Autumn in the Mountains," "White-throated Sparrow, "Tea"; *Off the Coast:* "Death on a Bicycle"; *Beloit Poetry Journal:* "Borscht," "How Reb Katzman Got to Heaven"; *Ibbetson Street:* "What the Sparrow Said"; *Hunger Mountain:* "Last Things"; and *The American Poetry Review:* "Wait."

"A New Life" was reprinted in *From A to Z: 200 Contemporary Poets*, ed. David Ray (1981), and "Severed Heads" was reprinted in *Anthology of Magazine verse & Yearbook of American Poetry* (1995/1996. "Collateral Damage" appears in *Bagels with the Bards, No. 2*, ed. Molly Watts. "Reflections in a Furniture Store Window" will appear in a forthcoming anthology of Indiana Poetry, *And Know This Place*, ed. Jenny Kander & Charles Greer (Indiana University Press). "Testament" will soon appear in *Salamander*. "Buffalo, 1938" will appear in the anthology *Bagels with the Bards, No. 4*. "Should Lotty Leave Home?" "Lotty Calls Me," "Borscht," and "A Little Poem" appeared in a chapbook—*Silk & The Ragpicker's Grandson* (Red Dust, 1998).

My friends, some living, some now dead, have also been friends of my poetry—but these especially: Lysander Kemp, Gene Magner, Alan D'Arcangelo, Vry Carscadden, Fred Paddock, Bob Nichols, Kevin Bowen, Bruce Weigl, John Anderson, Sue Roberts, Kim Garcia, Franny Lindsay, Henry Braun, Michael Mack, Etheridge Knight, Harris Gardner, and Taylor Stoehr. Warm thanks to all of them, and to the gang in Brookline. Thanks also to the Somerville Arts Council for a grant that helped me complete this project.

ISBN 0-9795313-8-1 / 978-0-9795313-8-5

# TABLE OF CONTENTS

*For my* mispuchah—*Tam, Erika, Anna, Peter, Sandy—*
*and to the memory of Rachel and Lotty*

Steerage was the place deep in the hold, well below deck, windowless, where, for centuries, they put cattle that had to be carried across the ocean. When the great waves of migration came to the U.S., the thousands of dirt-poor peasants rode there as well. "Down there," asks Bert Stern's ancestor in the title poem of *Steerage*,

> Who knew
> where to go to the toilet, if there would be water?
> In a corner, on blankets, we made house.

The crowding, the noise, the "smells of stale / seawater and piss, animals and human sweat," made the gorge rise. One woman called it Gehenna, hell, but they all went down into the hold anyway and most of them made it to America. That's where this remarkable book of poems starts, with such memory as Stern can piece together, or imagine, of what brought his ancestors, driven out of Russia by pogrom, to a life in Buffalo.

> All suffered to bring me here to this room
> where I write, bigger than the house
> my mother was born in.

"I am somebody's dream. Let them/ tell me if they can . . . if I am recompense for what they endured."

"Steerage" also plays on the verb, to steer, to guide. This is the defining act of these poems. In the long absence of those who "suffered to bring me here," late in life, with death almost a friendly companion, the poet moves gingerly but expertly between his fears and longings, between then and now. "Myself," he says in "Blackberries," "I don't go back much further / than last Tuesday's two a.m.,

> but I smell my elders almost benign
> around me, and I eat the berries
> they send forth as seed.

In "A New Life," the speaker finds that his old cast-off life doesn't (perhaps can't) go away. He had given his herring-bone tweed jacket, emblem of that old life, to the Salvation Army, but accidentally left in its pocket a post card addressed to him. On it, the words, "I'm glad to be without you, you never did me good." The new owner, a stranger, shows up on his door step one day. "Severance is real, he told me when he came, / attention must be paid."

I paid it. I took him in.
We live like severed lovers,
in separate unmade beds.

In like fashion, these poems make a new life out of many severances.

More than anything else, Bert Stern's poems find a way to wear the great heaviness of life with a charitable lightness. In a rare comic moment, a rabbi approaches the speaker asking for a donation to SPEJS, the Society for the Permanent Elimination of Jewish Suffering. "I gave already at the office," says the speaker. "What office?" "I can't explain. It's outside history." "Only God is outside history," says the rabbi, but wanting proof anyway, he takes off his black coat and fake beard and slips them over the speaker. "You can show me now," says the rabbi trickster. Stern, too, emerges as his own self-made rabbi (in a long tradition, it would seem), oracle or exegete of that sacred place outside history where the dead go and the dying long for.

One of the most moving poems of this collection, "Wait," placed next to last, tells of Jacob who sat by a girl, a girl who "was dying in his heart," the soul you might say of Jacob himself, to whom he says, "Wait . . . Listen. He knew a thin song that birds steer by." And Jacob sings it slowly, easing the girl, himself, the girl and (or as) himself, out of the world by recalling it.

God is sleeping but He is coming.
Now. Wait.
Remember a leaf.
Remember the turnip's sweet spheroid,
its little tail.
Say how stars live, burning.
How the stony icicles of this grotto live,
drip, drip, as if breathing.

Fire and ice. And, yet, as he says in "Testament," "Even now children are being born." Or, in "White-Throated Sparrow":

Always a white-throated sparrow
singing on a mountaintop, and somebody
there listening to it for the first time.
That's what you need to believe . . .

The survival manuals don't tell us how to survive life itself, the harness of daily living, the distance between ourselves and what we hope for. This is why *Steerage* is a book to cherish.

–Roger Mitchell

STEERAGE

*Oy, Gott,* send me a little poem,
you'll never miss it.
Sweet *gottenyu!*
You know how I could use it.
Not Paradise Lost or the book of Job I'm asking,
only something normal,
a little poem proper to me.

I want voices of things chattering in it
like it has rolled around with the earth a while.
Let it smell of something,
smoked fish, a woman's skin,
a *gedile mid grivn,*
red wine under the nose
just before you drink.

Did I ask to hear the earth thumping in it,
like on the third day?
Or for peace, happiness, justice,
the wicked withering away?

No, a little poem only,
to watch water flowing through rocks,
fishes still in the current,
geese flying over,
noisy, like children.

PART I: CHANGING PLACES

Six apples my mother bought on the pier and wrapped in her shawl with
   things we'd need every day.
The things that we didn't—three linen napkins, a handful of silver spoons
   my mother got from her mother
when she married—these we kept in a hamper with handles we'd
   schlepped up the steep plank.
Steerage stank, even before we went down iron stairs with no railing.
   Babies were crying.
We looked back to the top of the stairs: a woman stood, looking down,
   frozen. . . .*veh*, smells of stale
seawater and piss, animals and human sweat. *Gehenna* this woman cried.
   But the crowd pushed behind her
and she went down with the rest. Down there, at first, who knew where to
   go the toilet, if there would be water?
In a corner, on blankets, we made house: here, bundles to lean against,
   there, to keep garlic and bread,
sausages smelling of garlic, and just here, clean clothes to change into, as if
   clothes could make order.
At night I'd remember: in the market square Feter Joshua held me and said
   he would come—
in six months, no more. He talked to make order, he said what he hoped,
   as if God gave us life
as we want it. But order is like houses children weave from grasses, twigs
   and leaves.

The first morning, for breakfast, my mother and I shared an apple. I closed
   my eyes, and saw
the strong tower. I chewed as long as I could for the sweetness. When the
   ship rocked,
and over the thumping of engines the babies were crying
   and women and men.

crying to God for His mercy, I imagined America—Liberty like a tower,
   her torch,
father in a strong house, order. I said over and over,

>   *the Lord*
>   *is a strong tower*
>   *the righteous run into it*
>   *and are safe.*

Up on deck each day we went heavier, until nobody lifted their head
   up from steel plates of the deck
and grey winches. Nobody talked. We could not look at the sea
   or the dead sky
above us. We hung between these. We would be here always.

There was a bird I liked,
its name was I don't remember.
It skimmed the waves a day from shore.
My mother held my head up to the rail,
I was too sick to stand.

America, she said,
this bird has its nest in America.
I could fly as far as that bird flew,
my mother said, its wings are fragile feathers.

When the ship came into the harbor
my spirit was waiting for me,
dancing on the shore,
a bird on the edge of the water.

When the *muzhiks* came, her mother
was bent, dragging branches.
Avram gone more than a year,
in America, by a great lake.
Pulling dead branches over dirt
hard and spare as her life, she day-dreamed
America—no *muzhiks*.
Then the hooves and shouting.

A demon rode at her laughing,
in shiny black boots, baggy pants,
vest from wolves, swinging
his long knife over his head,
to slash her. Then, beyond terror,
she sees him bow his head and smile,
as a man might nod to a woman
on the village square. Then he's gone.
Back in her hut she sings to the babe in her belly
to soothe it.

Didn't want to be born, this child,
held herself back, upside down. Aunty
could not get her turned, afraid, mother
screaming, did God know what He was doing,
was *this* to be chosen, crying out
under leaden skies among enemies,
without meat, making soup from barley
and bad potatoes, maybe a shank bone?
For this the *muzhiks* had spared her,
God in his eye.

Yet the child *was* born and grew.
When she was five, her mother carried her,
on foot, in the back of carts, to Antwerp.
The child would be sick in the stinking hold,
such a fever. It seemed they would bury her
in the grey sea without *mitzvoth* to soften death,
who could remember the prayers?

But she lived and they came to the cheap flat
my *zeda* had found. All day he sold
vegetables and fruits from a cart.
At home he'd stopped speaking
except, to his children in the yard,
*stop playing, go inside,*
*you're wearing out shoe leather.*

His best memory was his mother
canning in the autumn: pickles from
cucumbers and watermelon rinds; plums
and cherries in thick preserves.
Each night in the fall in the basement
what he hadn't sold he peeled and sliced,
cooked, stuffed into jars and lined
shelves with relish, pickles, bright fruit,
wine from the grapes, and schlivovitz
from plums rich as the ones he picked
on the hills above Kishinev when he was a boy.
Evenings, at the kitchen table, he drank shlivovitz
alone, or sometimes tea with big gobs of jam,
or through sugar lumps, nobody near him.

But no *muzhiks* on Adam Street,
school for the children. My mother
who wanted not to be born grew up,

married, was my mother, suffered.
All suffered to bring me here to this room
where I write, bigger than the house
my mother was born in.

I am somebody's dream. Let them
tell me if they can—my mother and bubby,
Hannah, Avram who came
to America alone, a boy who knew nothing,
and even the *muzhiks* who held back the long sweep
of his knife—let them tell me if they can
if I am recompense for what they endured.

A gold star we embroidered
on black to lay over the coffin—
bright star, to shine under the dirt.
Then they took her away
on rough boards to the graveyard
while I hummed to myself
a song against death—
no tune, just a droning.

I stayed home with the women
to sweep away sorrow
till the men returned
with dirt on their hands
by a different road
so the ghost shouldn't follow.
They washed from the bowl
I held out, but I didn't watch them.

I watched the swallows nested under the roof,
birds that were noisy with spring.
I watched how the clothes
Tanta Leah had hung on a bush
still flapped in the wind.
Dust stirred in the yard.

By her grave we sang the psalm against death.
God would cover us with His feathers,
angels bear us up in their hands,
the lion and the adder we would trample.
But how could words or a washing
stand against death?

Death would pitch us into the dirt,
each in a hole, without stars.
Who knows what goes on down there
under that weight? *Shekinah* shines
till the end, even in darkness,
the old men say this, sipping tea—
shines in fragments like glass,
sharp pieces for Messiah to put back
where they should be, under God's light,
each whole in God's sight.

After two months
Father took me one day to the grave:
a marker of painted tin over wood,
the wood painted with oil paint
to keep it from rotting.

But my mother was under the earth.
They had washed her and wrapped her
in linen, white, without knots,
so when the time came, Messiah
could unwrap her and sweep her naked
back into the light.

Harold talked to me more than he had to,
I was just a typist. About cases he asked me
my advice and about his wife. Sometimes
I gave it, what did I know, I was a girl.
But too smart for a typist, he said.
So he'd stand by my desk, and once
he touched my hair. You're smart, Lottie,
you know what's going on. He would send me
to law school if I wanted. You'll make money
for me, you don't have to type, you're too smart
for this. I knew what he wanted but he meant it.
A chance he was giving me, my last chance.
He wanted I should live by myself, take a room.
I liked him. I didn't care. With my one short leg
nobody could like me. But I was wrong, and about
his wife we could see later. I was a good girl but I needed
to go out of the house where my father sat at the table
staring at his teacup and always we had to try to please him.
Us girls, we should be like servants. The young ones
he kept home after school to help my mother. Me,
I was smart, he let me out, to make money
for Maury's education. When I told my mother she
looked at me like I'd killed her. *Die Kinder* stopped
talking to me, they just stared.

Harold waited but he was sure. For himself
he had solved everything. His wife was a *shikker*,
all day she sipped wine like a lady but she
was a *shikker*. He came home to never any supper,
never something nice. Once alone in the office with me
he took out his thing and wanted me to touch it.

I ran out of the office and walked up and down Delaware.
I drank coffee in Woolworth's, then went home
like I'd been all day at work. Next day at the office
he was sorry. This didn't happen again. Weeks went by.
I told Harold, yes, almost ready. But I lied. At home
were the children, they knew nothing, who would teach them
the world? At home was my mother, brave to come to America
where every morning her Herschel thanked God aloud
He did not make him a woman. *Later,* I told Harold,
I will come to you *later. Nu,* later didn't come. Crying,
my mother came to my room every night to beg me and
tell me she would die. She hadn't even talked to my father.
They couldn't stop me. All I had to do
was put my clothes in a bag
and walk out the door.

Evenings that went on forever
still unfolding. Deep Buffalo
winter, living room soft auburn,
daddy asleep on his back, evening
*News* over his face, mother
knitting in her chair, reading
the book on her lap, I at her feet,
reading. Silence. I can hear
our breathing.

PART 2: SPRING AND FALL

Four crows in silhouette
pass over the tulip tree
while I unload the trunk
of groceries in plastic bags—
broccoli, a ham,
jar of cherry jam,
a watermelon
proud of its seeds,
leeks, sophisticates,
pastel green and white,
keeping their dirt inside
as we do.

As I cross the yard,
rope scrap hanging
from maple limb
hootchy-kootches
in the wind.

As for me, I take pills to breathe,
pills to be happy, but, still,
spitting venom, snakes rise
from brown paper bags
in my dreams.

So I praise the four crows,
buzzards riding thermals,
squirrel lice, and the squirrel
on the maple limb,
scratching her gold grey haunches in pale sun
with a rear foot that drives like a piston.

Falling bodies clutch
one another aglow
like chestnuts open
to the skin, fluids
rising menstrual.
Tender skin of river stones,
plum skin, flecked pear,
pocked avocado, stars
with their skins on fire,
grape skin clinging
to pulp, egg skin
cradling yolk, your
skin to my skin.

*   *   *

Even before their first embrace
children can smell that passion
comes to this.

Out in the meadow
we'll burn in the brush pile,
glad to be smoke at last
and come back as ghosts
children will see
just when stars come out.

The wind sounds like your voice,
furious, indifferent.

You probably want to go to bed,
but I keep making a racket, prattling
to the moon. O borrowed brightness,
cup of peace, container for owls and
hooting bears, O silversmith
scattering bright earrings in empty fields
and upon the waters of wilderness,
shaper of owl light that I return
more tender for my wrappings.

A local history of the empty
in this flapping flag against a sky
alive with heroic, sailing cumulus
over a running track whose
lane lines converge toward
where I sit at a library window
above a crumbling university
one might take for a symbol
if it weren't for the actual
falling brick. "To end
the day in tiny affirmations,"
says Susan Howe to someone,
I think me, "affirmations
made sitting in night attire."
I catch the nodding poet's bent.
I sniff her scent.

Sal snores deep and steady.
Her pups suckle.
The ones cast out from the teat
softly whine demands.

The fire's grown quiet.
Cold rises from my own feet.
I rise to stir the stove.

Inside the open stove
a bustling city glows.
Who knows how to live there?

A pup nips my ankle,
I stumble over another.
Sal's breath is figured bass.

The miller got tired of grinding.
Everywhere, the sacks were full, leaking
yellow or white, everywhere
the mice fat on their gleanings.

What would they do with more bread,
the women, hands ghostly
with flour? Who cared for the cakes,
so much sweetness, to sicken the children?

But autumn had come and the miller
must grind. Something was grinding the leaves
and the flowers, cold womb drying up,
earth recoiling its juices.

I

The sister rides, her brother leads the mule
through rutted mud that glints with silicon.
Her legs are bare. Her brother loves her dearly.
He takes her to the market like a lady,
where she will touch fruit with her
small fair hands.

His own hands are leather, and his linen shirt
hangs loose as he walks bent, patient, intent.
Here and there, ripe apples, squirrel-bitten,
perfect, lie under the trees.

He lets the horse eat. Half prone
along the horse's neck, his sister sings
a song that knows what her heart wants
and lets it rise like a flight of doves
up from her belly.

2

At the harvest market, to the loud tunes
of hucksters, they meet friends, chat,
he hangs around, but she, purposive,
goes off to buy two turnips, potatoes,
a melon, parsnips, a little meat.
A tinker clatters new pans,
making them sing.

Let her stop at a bin of black pearls,
precious and rare and see
how they send back, as through scrim,
images that light upon each separate pearl.
With her small hand, she plucks one up
and looks closely at the passing real.
Her own face is there. She studies it,
and then, assured, returns the pearl
to the bin.

Let's say her brother's drinking ale
with other herders. Nobody minds
the flea-bitten dogs under the rough
pine table. For talk, they have only
the sun on their faces and foreknowledge
of how soon summer will be over and the ground
turn hard and wolves come down at night,
sniffing after the livestock.

The brother's hands are cured like hide
by dirt and sun. With these others, he spends
summers herding goats on upland meadows,
sculpting himself out of the weights
he lifts and lugs, out of high slumber
under fierce wind, and first dawns
at a fire, drinking bark tea.

## 3

I join him to drink tea with shadows
I've awakened, seated on cold ground,
a blanket still wrapped round me.
My own time is a scream.
There's something I'm trying
to remember. Some common love,
lost, hides in the texture of linen,
or glances at me out of a pearl.

This morning, otherwise idle,
I stir milk into sunlight.
At once, the maple leaves
seem to come from another planet
though they sigh to me as before,
roused by wind and as real as my fingers.

I hear the steady screaming
as loud as you do, but I'm old
as the sun and feather light,
hardly hatched, my toy wings
damp with yolk. You may
have heard, the Pope sold me
in pieces as relics. This is
an exaggeration.

But tread lightly when you tread
on me. Ask if you may let your
breath fall on me, and ask politely.
Like everyone, I'm made of stars
and birds, the leaves of trees.

Today the spare book opens
　　to mountains and cold air.

Chickadees mind their business
　　of feeding and flitting,
leaving behind their rusty sounds
　　and one-note cries.

Still lurking behind the ridge
　　the sun considers evening
though it's hardly nine A.M.
　　On my page
the only green is evergreen.

Early this morning, while you
still clung to a chapter of sleep,
deer stepped out of their book
　　of tree shadow
and ate fermented apples under the tree.
Then the dogs sent them away
　　and wakened you.

Mealtime with its little ceremonies. Listening to one another across
the table. Trying not to gnash too bestially. Taking the other in,
the good sight of her, the long habit of seeing. Features. Fine com-
plexion, clear eyes. Over soup. Over *tortillas con queso,* baked.
Paprika on them, or a bit of scallion. Olives on them. Toward the
end of lunch the dog stirs to the prospect of plates. We make plans
toward the end of lunch, we are free, we shape our days. Last
night's bad dreams are smoke.

Others gulp sandwiches while talking on the phone. They don't have
time to pee. I speak only of the favored ones, not the ones who
gulp down candy bars on the plant floor to the roaring of
machines. Nor of the ones who skip meals out of need, or eat tortillas with nothing to put on them. I don't speak of those—they're
everywhere—who eat nothing at all and grow gaunt and can't
speak to each other because they have nothing to say, they are
starving. I don't speak of the beasts of the woods—the deer in
their spring grazing, the fisher feasting on porcupines and house
cats. I don't speak of seeds, of leaves gorging, or plant stems
straining upward for light and roots down, for the dark.

When we lie dying we lose interest in eating. *Eat this, ma, you need
the strength.* No, she does not. *We need to build you up.* But no,
though she feels it, the strain her son places on her, *Stay alive,
ma, don't leave us now.* Still, she does try, perhaps owes this to
him. But her gesture is hollow, and the food he offers sawdust in
her mouth. So she passes, no longer to eat, enters the darker chapter, to be eaten. But best not think of this. We are eating lunch
here. In one another's eyes, the dailiness of love. Outside our window, mountains sport nap of oak and pine.

Always a white-throated sparrow
singing on a mountain top, and somebody
there listening to it for the first time.
That's what you need to believe,
at least, as your eyes stroke the ruffled
nap of the peak across the valley
and you hear that sweet call again,
as final as it ever was, leaving nothing
to say beyond the five notes of its saying.

Hooves beating on sand, brilliant,
monotonous gurgling of water over rocks
—a philosophy woven of quiddities.

In the noonday sun even sparrows
sound asleep. Wild vines bedizen
garages tear-stained with tar.

Yoked, oxen are given nowhere to go
and look bewildered—but not at me.
I did not invent the arresting power
of sensations heard or remembered.

Singer of water and sky, say
the swimming swan made this up,
or a kestrel falling out of the blue.

What I can't name keeps a photo album,
abhors moving pictures. Explosions
of the sun are pasted there in single frames.
Now, turn the page. Pathos of lily
unfolding is killing.

But who can freeze-frame the weather?
Cloud exposes itself like Salome,
slow veil by slow veil, down to
a swan, a mist, and a forgetting.

# BLACKBERRIES

*for Hans Heinzerling*

I bushwhack down lean deer trails
that lead me in the wrong direction,
trudge logging roads that haven't known
a wheel or hoof for a hundred years
but carry me a while, then turn into
mountain laurel and leave me flat.

Inside the things I walk among
a kind of silence reigns that lets me
hear a deerfly's furious scherzo, an
old oak's creak, mosquito's whine,
a bird's quick notes of warning.

Boulders are saying nothing
as they always did, but they
remember the glacier's rough
shoulder of earth and ice that
pushed them here and left.
Taller than trees, their dignity
derives from memory, and even
modest stones remember: *Long*
*before glacier we were fire.*

All sweat and itch and heavy breathing
half tangled in hobble bush and blackberry,
I walk in a midst I reach by way of
scant footholds and blessed pine roots
to cling to.

Myself, I don't go back much further
than last Tuesday's two a.m.,

but I smell my elders almost benign
around me, and I eat the berries
they send forth as seed.

Back in a then so long ago there was nothing to look back to
and the long ride to Charley's farm in Ontario was an adventure,
we were happy in the car, Mother singing songs of longing
that *she* looked back to from when she was a child in the war,
and the long, long roads a-winding pointed to the peace
we had now, there in the car, before the new war came on,
and Daddy happy driving, getting lost to see what he could see,
though we'd all beg him to go by the map, and my sister and I happy
to see them happy so we'd sing along, oh, *Keep the home fires*
*burning, while our hearts are yearning,* for the feeling,
not knowing yet what people longed for in long wars, but free,
on the road, and though I'd sometimes get car sick my mother
would give me a lemon to suck on and then I'd be okay, back then
I'd see road signs that called out, *Eat* or *Hot Food,* and because
we'd never stop, hot food seemed to me mysterious, particular,
food that I'd never eaten but naturally yearned for.

Later, in another time, driving through the night
   to the City from Buffalo
with Gita Nonni in a four-door convertible in December
   without a heater
and only a blanket over our laps to keep us warm and singing I can't
remember what but probably the lovely songs Susanne Bloch
sang to her lute, or songs the Wobblies sang, I learned that hot food
was open turkey sandwiches with mashed potatoes and delicious
floury gravy, hold the over-cooked peas. We'd had our own war by
then, and after that war came new hot foods, pizza, egg foo yung,
   vegetables cooked right.
But it isn't the food I am trying to get at as much as time, time that
has carried me past so many shoals and rapids, so many songs and
   tears and wrongs,

so many sweetnesses and Look!-We-have-come-throughs
to this Now, lavish with the so-much-to-look-back-to.

At the top of Spruce Hill,
just before the highway
plunges into the valley,
the wide sweep of mountains
gathers me in to its shadow
and silence, holds me,
until I am ready to fall
with the turnings of poplar
and oak. Through the windshield,
even the thin rain that takes on
gold light from the sun in its falling
is fuel for the burning.

That clear song—
was it you while I slept,
slipping down in your jade
silk to feed the stove
with pine and drink your tea
alone, at dawn, as you like to do?

PART 3: HOW REB KATZMAN GOT TO HEAVEN

*for Fred Paddock*

1. *The Rebbe Stops Talking*

Katzman's hair was tangled with sticks,
he'd forgotten how to talk. Where he ate
bread on the stoop of his hut, birds pecked
for crumbs. Raw boletus he gnawed
by the fallen oak where he picked them.

In sleep he flew like a night bird,
but, awake, language was a skin rash
that never went away.

*Words redden the skin of things,*
he sang to the wren at the door.
*I soothe them with silence I gather*
*until prayer cries out from my bones.*
*But words buzz like flies in swarms,*
*Oy, Adonai, strike down these burning angels*
*that guard Eden's gate.*

## 2. *Katzman at the River*

Oy Rebbe, oy Rebbe, the salmon said,
stippled, half water,
more light than flesh,
oy Rebbe, come in.

Katzman looked down.
Reflections of plum blossoms
floated on current, and in air
plum branches tossed in the noon light.

Katzman washed his clothes in the river
and hung them on branches of plum.
As he slid down the bank on his tuchus
great drops splashed into the sun,
and he swam and sang praises.

### 3. *April Storm*

Katzman kept a garden, worked each clod
in his hands until the roots of the weeds
came loose. Soil fell in pellets
and he raked it fine with a stick,
till the bed was a bed he might lie in.

But all night rolling thunder
and spears of fire with walls of rain
declared the Rebbe flimsy as a moth.
The storm would beat his beds
to mud by morning.
Katzman sighed, bowed by law.

## 4. *Shabbes*

Reb Katzman came out of the woods to go to *shuel*
but outside the synagogue people turned from him
because he smelled like a beast.
Even the children laughed behind their hands
to see his beard and hair entangled with twigs.

Katzman had lived too long with spirits,
but what could he do?
Tell children that the dead own the world
and we must do what we can to please them?

## 5. *Katzman's Tears*

The Rebbe woke ill to hear
the ravens call to one another
across the winter meadow. The birds
made the wild weight of the world
without him personal, talking
as if he weren't there.

Leaves on the trees
and on the shy stems of the flowers
said the same thing.
They would go on talking for a long time
in the half light of his absence,
patient in their goings and their comings.

Earth took in his tears like rain.
Some drops were drawn to the sun.
Katzman prayed he might die
in the arms of whatever might hold him,
Maybe God would come later.

## 6. *Trayfe Katzman*

Young and full of spirit, what could Katzman do?
Stay home nights
to watch his mother sweep,
the girls at her apron strings,
father *davening,* snoring,
mumbling tales from the Talmud?

No. Katzman went to the tavern
to drink and sing with the Poles.
He'd fight and get bloody,
go off with a girl.
Shikse? *Mox nix.*
Drunk he came home
and drunk he slept.
When the sun rose he sawed boards
his father hammered into chairs and tables.

One night on a dare from the Poles
Katzman ate pork and he liked it.
Now a mensch, an old man who said his prayers
and loved God, Katzman prayed forgiveness.
And God said:
*Who keeps score? Just keep singing.*
Ah!
The law was the law,
but something better stood behind it.

## 7. *Katzman and the Ladies*

Katzman woke and dressed,
and praised the holy name in song.

The day was overcast,
sun darting in and out of clouds.

Then came the laughing voices—
women gathering mushrooms in the woods,

hair down and kerchiefs heavy with fruit.
They'd come near to hear him sing

and eat with him, boletus roasted on sticks,
and the bread they brought.

Then Katzman led their dancing in a ring.

## 8. *Katzman's Last Song*

The women came to be near him,
but, dying, Katzman was distant.
One night he called out,
help me sit, and they sat him.
When Katzman opened his mouth,
the women leaned close.
He sang, praising Eden,
then turned from it.

PART 4: LAST THINGS

This constant bear is heavy and here, rankness
like swamp water indistinct from mud bed, what
moves in water indistinct from mud. This moody bear
does not eat berries. His rankness dims a meadow
pale butterflies cross like petals.

I dreamed I could make him dance. Dance on a rope
if I had one, dance for a gypsy if I had one.
Dance and make money from ungainliness,
from lumbering weight, dancing undanceliness,
make the children laugh. If I had a gypsy.

From beginning to end God's mind is
this bear's mind. What could He ponder,
heavens, empty and void? The history of
all that must be and all that is holy,
whispering to himself?

No, wrapped in the bear's
embrace, divine breast pressed
against bear's breast,
God breathed bear's knowledge in:
no things and no words, nothing to say
or have heard, nothing to translate, only
to suffer this heavy bear—no *ipses* here,
no *quods*, nor *nuncs*, nor *claritas*,
no whelps,
no combs full of honey.

There was a burning on my skin.
There were red lines on my skin,
then my blood flowed in its channels.

I could not say why the gob of blood in my breast
throbbed like a drum. Reader, you would have asked,
*Why kidneys? Why lungs?* I had no brain.
I was spirit, stunned. Nobody said please
come into the world—I was woven.

This wasn't a sun I asked for.
I didn't know why the leaves come in their waves
or why a wave rolls through everything.
There was water rushing and the sound of water,
a wave beginning and a wave ending.
I didn't know that angels could get tangled
in the winter branches, or that the sun in winter
only seems to shine on an alien planet. All that I held
in my arms got broken until you came and I learned
that flesh could marry.

It is always like this. Even now children are being born.
They are sucking milk because they were made to,
and staring at their mothers from across a great distance.

Kenny's bad boy's across the street,
washing his car, a black Camarro
with V8 engine, white letter
tires, and Holly carbs,
just like his dad's.
Sundays, they both drive out
to car shows, but my show's
just out the window, where the cars
lie dreaming like black cats.

Around here, people *are*
their cars, even the heap
another father and son lie under
in their driveway chop shop
next door to Kenny's.

As for Angie, the kid
washing his Camarro, I know
his dirty little secrets. I saw him
on the avenue yesterday, outside
his car, laid back against the burnished
hood, telling a brown-skinned girl
to get in. Instead, she tossed
her black hair and walked away,
he still yelling as she moved
fast down the street, already
half a block away. For a moment
he froze in wrathful astonishment,
then, like a flash, his u-turn
trails stink of burnt rubber.
I saw him catch her, drag her in

almost before she could scream,
and they're off to where I don't
want to think about.

I know there's karma somewhere,
but across the street, as Angie wipes
a chamois over the car's flanks, his face
is open and innocent as a child's.
Watching him, I shake my head.
Maybe he'll get better as years
press down on him. Or maybe,
just now, he's touched as I am
by the clear sky of Mary's blue
hanging over us, as if to soothe
our frayed angers and heal
the bruised heart of the girl,
naked, defenseless against us.

Muffle the words,
gag the mouth.
Drive the heart crazy
with hunger for a story
to tell, any easy river
to drift down in a trance.

No, make the heart
walk the streets with a rice bowl,
its misery an iron mask. Let it
find what it seeks there.

In the furniture store window
TV plays all night. People are in their beds,
even the bad boys who ride skateboards
and the girls who press against them
in the bank's empty parking lot,
looking bad in black dresses, faces
painted white to light somebody's way
into dark places—they all will sleep
in fugitive beds, under someone else's sheets.

This is the hour when, in the store window,
the television plays all night that ghosts may hear
race car drivers preach motor oils.
The ghosts also like violence and sex,
and people opening wide their spigots
until ooze pours out like tar, and an
audience swills it down like Stroh's Light.

The ghosts are neither happy nor unhappy.
They are ghosts, they have nowhere else to go.
They don't know the difference between fast foods
and beer ads, and they are not sure if news
is different from these, or from the singers
who moan inconsolably.

Far beyond them, the girls in black
who trail in the dreams of skateboarders
could tell the ghosts what's what,
but they finally sleep,
and float without abrasion.
Their dresses of skin

shimmer like light, and the
sleeping boys, not hungry anymore,
don't need skateboards to glide
and glide on purple seas under a
purple sun, until a deeper current
carries them to shore,
and not even television
interests them any longer.

Summer ended. We packed up, we packed it in.
Tomorrow might have been another day, but now, not.
We wrapped things tight, in throbbing packages.
We packed the room in, and stashed it in a matchbox.
She said, there's nothing much to do
with the sea wind ruffling the curtains
I said, leave the clouds alone, they belong here.
Back and forth about the sky and weather.
What shall we do with the children?
Not pack them off to camp, but pack them into boxes
like machine gun slugs.
We whispered names, faith, hope, charity,
that sounded like wind sighing.
We wrapped ourselves in see-through plastic grocery bags.
There were words lying all over the floor.
We swept them in a pile and rolled the rug.

Sitting at the screen again, I'm Penelope
working at the winding sheet. Then Death
bursts in, abustle with business. "Let's
get out of here," he says, "we need
fresh air." In no time, from the foot
of a mountain, we're scrambling
over rocks and roots, we're hauling
ourselves, he light as air, I paunchy,
half-winded. We stop to look
at spring violets. He breathes
the spring air in deeply, he pounds
his chest. On the peak, he can't
stop talking about the vastness
of the view. He says, "it's like
being in heaven."

Afterward, Death and I take
counter seats at the diner.
We're eating BLTs.
"A great sandwich,"
he keeps saying. He sips
his coffee black, cup after
cup. "So I'll stay up late,"
he says, with a wink, then adds,
"Truth be told, I never sleep."
You can see it on the sides
of trucks I take to battle fields
to haul away my part of the dead:
"Death Doesn't Sleep, we're
there for you 24/7." I've thought
of sending out fliers: "Let us

take you gently into the night."

"Why don't you just shut up?"
I ask. He's hurt and sulks
a while in silence, then orders
one more coffee. "How about
Death on a Bicycle?" And I say,
"What the hell." We peddle round
the parking lot while he's learning gears,
then we hit the mountain roads
where he's so happy I wonder
if he might retire. Later,
he's gone and I in my bed alone,
reflecting on the day, such fun.
And how about Death, so open
to life, so exquisitely ready
to savor?

Albert limps, sheepish, into my poem.
I'm glad to see him though.
His hair's combed like Hitler's
but more wet. He still wears
the herringbone tweed jacket
I gave to the Salvation Army.
That's how we met. He found a card
in the breast pocket addressed to me.
It said:

*I'm glad to be without you,*
*you never did me good.*

It made him sad, he said,
like severance always did.

But he was half-buried in troubles
of his own and years went by, the card
snug in what was his breast pocket now,
chafing, sometimes, he said,
like a slight contusion.
It was the drift of things,
he said, that carried him to me
over hard miles and several years.
He liked the coat
but thought I ought to have the card.
Severance is real, he told me when he came,
attention must be paid.

I paid it. I took him in.
We live like severed lovers,

in separate unmade beds.
I cook. He somehow pays the bills.

# OCTOBER, 2002

*for Taylor Stoehr*

Truth never flew lower than this—
down the block, a slow hammer
pounding, low clouds that press us,
flat, and leaves in their last turning.
Slow start of this bad winter.

My dear ones who used to laugh
now weep and hunker down.
Sad days for the republic.

Down the block
a man keeps hammering.
Bravo, his steadiness, his mere
raptapatap.

Framed in his open door and screened
by maple limbs, with their loads of melting snow,
Kenny steps out to check the mail.
I hardly see him anymore—not through
the study window that is my frame,
nor in the street, neighbor to neighbor.

No, Kenny's going down. With his bad
knees, big belly, and sniper hallucinations.
Last night he called me to explain
his friend had just come over
and taken his sniper's rifle away.
"Listen," Kenny said, "my son-in-law
shows up but when I look at him I see VC."

When the phone rang, I'd been watching snow
melt from his pitched roof, remembering
how carefully he pruned his pear tree in the fall,
raked the leaves, put up a porch display and flag
for every holiday. But Kenny's going down,
with his big heart and gift of gab, he's falling
out of the neighborhood,
one piece at a time.

I'm listening to him on the phone and in a flash,
I'm on patrol, tangled in jungle and high on opium.
I'm walking in Kenny's fearful shoes
shooting at shadows and sure my next step
will land smack down on a *punji* stake
or box full of scorpions.

I watched him
frame a window once, and, eyes closed,
I watch him still—sizing boards with a handsaw,
setting them snug. When he saws
his saw sings. In spring, his hammer rings.
But in his dreams, he shoots a girl,
hardly a shadow—shoots her every night.

How they stink through their final days
and babble out of deep meditations,
entangled in tubes, synthetic liquids
broiling in their blood, and they without tears
to return to us, as we watch in white rooms.

Already gladly beyond us, they suffer
now this last transitory humiliation,
where love cannot reach, even as the body,
nearly dirt, clings to what it knew
of light and shade.

Late afternoons on the porch, we pull
on Canadian ale and watch the sun drop
behind a peak. Close at hand, as the wind
stirs through the dry stalks of summer
that remain in the rocky meadow
the mountains turn somber,
and last light touches us as they might touch.

In this waiting between cold rains,
across my neighbor's back yard,
frozen into sodden gestures,

white underwear and a string
of blackened work clothes
hang motionless, dejected.

Ah. Now let the deep gloom
of the sky settle on me without
offense, and cast off into the weather.

It doesn't matter what you think,
the sparrow said it first:
time will beat your heart away,
it all has been rehearsed.

The river's fist bangs down the dam,
sweet air is fouled with dirt,
my woman's gone, she won't come back,
America's accursed.

Who knows why my heart's so full,
why, old, I feel so fed?
Four times the sparrow at my feet
humps his twitching bride.

At night, space breathes in on me
and throws its flashing stars,
chanting chorus with waning moon,
you're ours, you're ours, you're ours.

In some yesterday, furies told me
the grass would grow through yawning
vacancies between my bones
until my bones stopped clanging
and forgot their names.
How could I keep from laughing?
Still they persisted. Aurora borealis
would glow from my memory of
a mouth, roots grope through to
my secret body and lap my final juices.

But I was drunk with flesh. Who isn't?
Each night before I slept I praised
the legs that carried me to you, praised
my arms when they held you.
Night and morning, my body swelled
with joy in breathing in and out
as I knew I always would do.

Never mind how my hair fell out and
my clattering teeth followed. Events,
yet not events to make me waver.
I still refused to listen to the owl
and what it knows. Yes, gray dissolute
fungi spawn with great appetites,
and worms ease our dissolution back to dirt.
Yes, burning maws in space erased my name.
But I, I, I knew that everything was mine.

\*   \*   \*

Tonight, nurses come and go, reading
my vital signs. Alarms go off like bells
to toll the dead. Sickness makes me
simple at last. Tonight, my roommate
coughed up a final word like a bone
and nurses bustled in, while I lay
in my muted bed, afraid
that I'd heard him correctly
and it was my word too.

All these naked ladies on Court Street
with their hands out like razors
supplicating, thighs brushing
together like scissor blades,
and hair dismembering as the wind.
All these naked ladies on Court Street
teach us. We smile back to the sun,
we celebrate birthdays, we bend,
breathing softly, over our softly
breathing infant daughter in her crib.
Then we put on the small airs that waft
us through the streets on somebody else's
business, while we wait to be found.
*Steer me, steer me,* flutters from us,
board me and steer me, for I'm adrift
in my life. The naked ladies on Court Street
come and go with the wind. When the sun
falls on their flesh they glow, and on cold nights
they glitter like foil under the moon.

While the boy stands by, restless,
sifting his eyes this way on that
over the barren rock, the old man
swings his ax, murmuring to himself
God's promises. His part? *Only walk*

*before me and be perfect.* Now
perfection rests in killing the boy,
hilarious surprise of Sarai's old age
and his own.

The air on fire before the fire is lit,
Abraham trembles and chokes, but
swings his ax, again, again, against
the dead pine branch. When he's
done, he gathers the scattered logs,
stacks them in the boy's outstretched
arms, grasps his knife and a burning
brand, and they climb.

Halfway up the goat path the boy
wonders and asks: the fire we have
and the wood, and the bright knife
in your hand, but where is the lamb
for this offering? Even after the old
man ties him to a tree and places
the logs around, even as he raises
his arm to plunge the knife into
the boy's breast, the absurdity of
this is impossible. How could God

want it, yet He bends the old man's
head to stony necessity.

And though the angel comes now,
in the flash of the blade coming down,
and the ram comes, horns caught
in a thicket, it is too late already.
In his heart, Abraham has killed
his only son, and though later
he is fruitful and multiplies,
and knows great mercy and
loving kindness, he walks bent
by the blow God smote him with
under stark skies, on a mountain
altar, his knife raised and the
cascading weight of everything
crashing down, to leave him
broken there, complete and alone,
bent by perfection.

A rabbi comes to the door—old school, in beard and caftan.

"?" I said.

He represented SPEJS, pronounced *shpay-chus,* he explained. "This is an acronym" Our mission is the Permanent Elimination of Jewish Suffering. This is what our society works for—*shpaychus.*"

"I'm sorry, I gave already at the office."

"What office?" the rabbi asked.

There *is* an office and I gave there. But told him, "I can't explain. It's outside history."

"Outside history?" the rabbi said. "*Goyishe Kop,* only God is outside history. Time is the river we swim in."

"It's a still place," I said. "I found it. It's outside history. An office there."

"So show me," said the rabbi.

"How can I show you? I'm not a rabbi."
The rabbi took off his black coat and insisted that I put it on. The rabbi took off his beard—aha, a trick beard!—and slipped the elastic over my head. "Okay, buster," the rabbi said, "you can show me now."

In my fur coat I'm walking in Buffalo like a sea lion.
Nobody makes good borscht anymore, how they used to do.
So I'm walking to the last store in America that sells
sour salt. But on such a day! The coat's warm but the snowflakes
    make me dizzy.
More of them than of me,
I keep losing my place.

When I left the house I had two blocks to go,
one short, to Mrs. Sunshine,
corner Commonwealth and Tacoma,
but now I've been walking all my life,
and still I am moving backwards.

When I began, I smelled pickles in the two barrels,
the old and the new ones, just a *bissel* schmaltz
herring in the air, and Mrs. Sunshine's knife
cutting through the halavah was gritty to the ear.
Oy, I am lost.
From here to Sunshine's delicatessen the people on the upstairs
porches, where in the summer time they swing on the glider
under the awning and listen to the elm trees,
those people are all dead, and the weakness is overtaking me as well,
this blinding snow, *verfleugete* winter without end.

PART 5: WAIT

The girl was dying in his heart,
where there were no palm trees,
no mild blue consolations.
Jacob didn't know what to say to her.
Fish scales shimmer in the depths
where no one sees them.
Tendrils of quiet sea forms
wave in the current, imagining food.
The girl's hair was pasted with sweat.
Her unlived life was a scream in her.


Water, Jacob said, its quiet voice.
She nodded, though words could not
hold her from her descent or lighten
the shady figure as it drew her gently
toward the blind stone mouth
that swallows the dead.


Wait, he said, listen. He knew
a thin song that birds steer by. Wait,
he said, I'll sing it. The rain falls
in torrents, coats the earth with
its own sheen, under the reflected
lights of stars. Wait, taste water.
It is a cold night. Pull the covers up,
press your body against whatever will hold it.

Jacob brooded like a dog looking for a place to piss.
His nose pulled him this way and that.
Sometimes he lingered for a long time,
riding pathways of molecules into memories
without images. But still he did not piss,
did not leave his mark. When the place
of places presented itself, it was not
something that he chose. It was a destiny.
For the instant of being there
he was home and home. His ecstasy
poured out of him in a yellow stream.


The day was brilliant but outside
his window. Here was another day
and he was in it. The day is a stage set,
he wrote. For another play, not the one
he was in, where the water he sipped
was words and his sipping was words.
Scraps of papers scattered on the desk
were words, and so were the books,
though the dust jacket of one had
been torn from a shopping bag, and
the Gideon Bible was bound
in tessellate plastic he liked to run
his fingers over. The book
speaking through his fingertips,
frightening him as if he had awakened
in a room full of people remote as stars.
But they were speaking, and then they were
shouting and chopping each other's heads off.
They were marching on hot sand without hope
and nailing each other to crosses. They knew
how to praise, but mostly they prayed for mercy.

So much blood everywhere, but here and there
a thin song that soared, long and trailing,
like the flight of a bird about to land
on the sweetest branch in the woods, in
a season different from the four ones that we know.
Of course she was still dying.
Jacob could feel her breath,
but she was far from him
in a darkness that kept deepening.
He called out to her as one might
throw a flower at a star.


He sat listening. There was nothing. She was too far and
   she was falling.


His tallis wrapped around him,
Jacob was saying *yisgadal v'yiskadash,*
while the dog next door kept barking,
and then another one across the street.
Each dog would say a few words, then wait.
The conversation was desultory from the start
and then it stopped. Jacob went downstairs and
put on his coat. Outside, he took his own dog for a walk.


   Walking he thought:
   The monarchs have gone south.
   Leaves feed the earth that fed them,
   grass lies dormant in autumn sun.
   I have no opinions.

*   *   *

High in the oak trees juicy air orchids grow.
Horses ate them when they fell. A line
of silent Indians walked past the pond
they called Pig Water, headed home
after buying meat and tequila. Behind them
a drunken gringo danced a jig and waved
a corkless empty jug like a baton. He kept
a crazy cadence. In fringed buckskin
he looked funny dancing like this
behind the drab and somber Indians.


To go down to the girl like that,
as part of a small procession,
drunk and dancing a jig. How
would her companion like that,
with his Mahler and Couperin,
his Russian novels?

*   *   *

The women who washed clothes
in the Pig Water had bare arms,
strong and brown. God made His
countenance shine on these women.
But they lived in straw houses
with no walls. Dogs and pigs ran in
and out over dirt floors. Daughters
awakened at dawn to start the fire
and make tortillas. God liked to hear
the pat-pat-pat their sleepy hands
made on the dough.

Sometimes God and Death together
sat listening to this.

But largely Death presided.
God watched from afar. Women
and their men drank aguardiente
in tumblers and their men walked
into people's houses and slashed
whoever came to the door
with bright machetes. God sighed
and let his mind become a river
thundering off mountains in the spring.
Men carried their new gashes and old scars
like birthmarks. The women went back
to the Pig Water to scrub clothes
on the rocks as before, the blood
from the men's shirts
drowning in muddy water.

*   *   *

The girl might be singing now.
She had stopped sweating
and a quiet had come over her.
There were stars out and
somewhere they were burning.
The sun was burning
somewhere in the dark.
But Jacob walked down a long
hallway carved from deep granite,
wet to the touch. The footing
was uncertain. Jacob heard music
farther on, a big orchestra,
without melody or harmony.

He thought: Each voice,
even when it is gone,
sings its own tune.

> *Little bird, little bird, where have you gone?*
> Deer grazed in old cornfields, looked up
> without fear, as if they heard singing.


Jacob remembered a piece of jade
carved to resemble a mountain.
a deep shaft cut into one side.
Little jade men went in and out of it.
The men coming out hauled skids
laden with great chunks of jade.
Men led horses, heavily laden
with jade heaped in saddle bags,
down a rocky trail.


*Yu.* The men coming down the mountain sang a song
that went:

> *Yu, heaven and earth meet in you,*
> *essence of water and hill.*
> *The emperor's girdle is studded*
> *with jade. We lay yellow jade*
> *on the altar of the earth, white*
> *on the altar of the moon.*

The words of the chant were carved into the base of the
mountain.

*If you had put a piece of jade in your mouth*
*as I told you to, this wouldn't be happening.*

The light goes out and leaves behind
a figure gowned and fragrant.
She has left her palace to sing songs
as kind as your mother's. You feel
her arms around you and you're safe.
Even now, at the door and about to leave,
she's close as your skin, still humming her tune.
Guests in the room hush for a moment and listen.


God sleeps in a deep crypt like this one, Jacob thought.
His sleep is some business only He understands.
We can't see what he is dreaming.


Not to be found again
but laid in the woods
among my bones.

Not to feel
sun touching my shoulder
your voice singing.

The wolves knew about this all along,
the snake said it was like this, like this.

Bright day no clouds,
my heart still beating.

Jacob was holding her and she felt like fire.
Death stood to the side, embarrassed.
The girl hugged Jacob with her weak arms.
She said now. She said this. The girl said this
now was always as it is now. She said the moon
keeps shining, there are seasons. Leaves unfold,
of course they do, and people pray and pray.
A child is throwing stones
at a stop sign, even now.
His pace rises in a slow toccata.
Under the frozen dirt
a tulip waits.


God is sleeping but He is coming.
Now. Wait.
Remember a leaf.
Remember the turnip's sweet spheroid,
its little tail.
Say how the stars live, burning.
How the stony icicles of this grotto live,
drip, drip, as if breathing.

# AFTERWORD

loneliness I am used to
down in the earth
you'd be surprised
chemistry has its own angers
the heart feeding parsnips

how happy I was
out back in the marigolds
and in the autumn over the gas burner
smell of tomatoes
and the plums in their loosened skins

my own skin you liked to touch shed now
as if flesh could comfort flesh because
it needs to
comfort me now
with your little memories
that fall to the earth like leaves
forgive me for not forgiving
you forgive this hopeless struggle
of the generations to be their own
for my not loving your father enough
how can anybody in that world you cling to
love anything against
the pile of bodies

what are we wanting all our lives
there is this great sadness burning in the blood
tenderness so fragile you saw how they took me
apart in pieces with their scalpels a voice continues
my needles when I was knittingthere was a beauty
in my face in the evening under the bridge-lamp
you saw it

"A Little Poem"
*Gottenyu : an affectionate diminutive for God*
*gedile mid grib*—literally, a good thing with chicken fat.
*noch:* untranslatable. In context of l. 5 rd: "It's not as if. . . ."

"Hannah Remembers"
*tanta:* aunt
psalm against death: Psalm 91
*Shekinah: the radiant presence of the Lord, as it scattered through the here-*
    *and-now.*
*mitzvoth*

"Lotty is Born"
muzhik: Russian peasant
*mitzvoth:* commandments and their performance

"Steerage"
*veh:* woe
*Gehenna:* hell
*Feter:* uncle

"How Reb Katzman Got to Heaven"
*Reb, Rebbe:* both words mean "teacher," or, sometimes, "spiritual master."
    "Reb" is used in conunction with a person's name.
*trayfe:* not kosher
mensch: stand-up guy
*tuchus:* rear end
*davening:* reciting Jewish liturgical prayers
*Shabbes:* Sabbath
*shikse:* gentile woman
*mox nix:* it doesn't matter

"Should Lotty Leave Home?"
*die Kinder:* the children
*shikker:* drunk, drunkard

"Bear"
*ipsi:* himself, herself, itself
*quod:* because
*nunc:* now
*claritas:* clarity, vividness, brightness

"Midrash: Changing Places"
*Goyishe kop:* gentile ways

"Borscht"
schmaltz herring: a kind of cured herring
*bissel:* a little bit
*verfleugete:* a word I coined

"Press Your Body Against Whatever Will Hold It"
*yisgadal v'yiskadash:* Opening words of the Jewish prayer for the dead

Bert Stern is Milligan Professor Emeritus at Wabash College and chief editor, retired, at Hilton Publishing. He and his wife, the poet Tam Lin Neville, co-edit a small press that publishes books by poets over sixty. For the past ten years, Bert has taught in CLTL, a program for people on probation.

Stern's essays and reviews have appeared in *Sewanee Review, Southern Review, Modern Language Review, Review Revue, Bloomsbury Review, The New Republic, Columbia Teachers' College Record, Adirondack Life,* and in a number of anthologies. His critical study, *Wallace Stevens: Art of Uncertainty,* was published by the University of Michigan Press in 1965.

Stern's poems have appeared in *Poetry, Hungry Mountain, Ibbetson Review, The American Poetry Review,* and *New Letters,* among others, and in a number of anthologies. His chapbook, *Silk/The Ragpicker's Grandson,* was published by Red Dust in 1998. Stern is the recipient of an artist's grant from the Somerville Arts Council.